I0889312

How Artists See HEROES

Myth History War Everyday

Colleen Carroll

ABBEVILLE KIDS

A DIVISION OF ABBEVILLE PUBLISHING GROUP

New York London

"Painters understand nature and love her and teach us to see her."
—VINCENT VAN GOGH

This book is dedicated with love to my darling daughter Isabel Hope . . .
you have made our family complete.

And to the heroes of September 11, 2001, who will never be forgotten.

My sincerest thanks to the people who helped me complete another volume in this series, especially Susan Costello, Jacqueline Decter, Patricia Fabricant, Paula Trotto, and my agent, Colleen Mohyde. A very heartfelt thank-you to Robert E. Abrams, who understood the concept for *How Artists See* from the beginning, and whose commitment to it helped the series improve with each volume.

And finally, to my amazing husband, Mitch Semel, for his unending support and encouragement. Okay, now we celebrate!

ALL MY LOVE, C

JACKET AND COVER FRONT: Palmer Hayden, *His Hammer in His Hand,* 1944–47 (see also p. 11).
JACKET AND COVER BACK, LEFT: The Boread Painter, Black-Figure Kylix, c. 570 B.C.–565 B.C. (see also pp. 4–5);
RIGHT: Jean-Auguste-Dominique Ingres, *Joan of Arc on Coronation of Charles VII in Cathedral of Reims,* 1854 (see also pp. 20–21).
JACKET BOTTOM: Winslow Homer, *The Life Line,* 1884 (see also pp. 32–33).

EDITORS: Susan Costello and Jacqueline Decter
DESIGNER: Patricia Fabricant
PRODUCTION MANAGER: Louise Kurtz

Text copyright © 2003 Colleen Carroll. Compilation, including selection of text and images, copyright © 2003 Abbeville Press. All rights reserved under international copyright conventions. No part of this book may be reproduced or utilized in any form or by any means, electronic or mechanical, including photocopying, recording, or by any information storage and retrieval system, without permission in writing from the publisher. Inquiries should be addressed to Abbeville Press, 137 Varick Street, New York, N.Y. 10013. The text of this book was set in Stempel Schneidler. Printed and bound in China.

First library edition
10 9 8 7 6 5 4 3 2

Library of Congress Cataloging-in-Publication Data
Carroll, Colleen.
Heroes : myth, history, war, everyday / by Colleen Carroll.
p. cm. — (How artists see, ISSN 1083-821X)
Summary: Describes the portrayal of heroes from myth, history, war, and everyday life, in various kinds of art.
Includes bibliographical references and index.
ISBN 978-0-7892-0773-9 (alk. paper)
1. Heroes in art—Juvenile literature. 2. Art appreciation—Juvenile literature. [1. Heroes in art. 2. Art appreciation.] I. Title II.
Series: Carroll, Colleen. How artists see.

N7760.C275 2003
704.9'42—dc21 2003045385

For bulk and premium sales and for text adoption procedures, write to Customer Service Manager, Abbeville Press, 137 Varick Street, New York, NY 10013, or call 1-800-ARTBOOK.

Visit Abbeville Press online at www.abbeville.com.

CONTENTS

BLACK-FIGURE KYLIX

Attributed to the Boread Painter

What makes a person a hero? Does a hero have certain qualities that most people lack? Can one become a hero simply by doing brave deeds, or does it take something more? In this book, you may find answers to these questions by seeing how sixteen artists depict heroes and heroism. Some of the heroes will be familiar to you, and others you will be meeting for the first time. Some of the heroes in the book lived many years ago, and others are living today. Some never lived at all, except in the myths and tales that tell of their remarkable exploits. Whether living or dead, man or woman, real or imaginary, the heroes on the following pages all possess something extra that just may exist in you, too.

Perhaps no other land in the world produced more heroes than Ancient Greece. Heroes abound in the Greek myths and legends, which take gods and goddesses, strange creatures, and even mere mortals on all sorts of exciting adventures. In this kylix, or cup, one such Grecian hero, Bellerophon, and his winged horse, Pegasus, fight a bizarre creature whose body is made from three different animals. Can you tell what animals it is made of? The artist placed his hero between Pegasus and the beast to draw your eye to him as he plunges his spear into the creature's belly. Why do you think the artist chose to show this particular moment in the struggle?

MYTH

STRUGGLE OF HERCULES WITH THE HYDRA OF LERNA

Francisco de Zurbarán

Here you see the most famous hero of all time, Hercules. In this picture, he battles another mythical villain, the nine-headed Hydra, or serpent. Armed only with a club and his super-human strength, Hercules is up against quite

a formidable foe. According to the myth, if one of the Hydra's heads was cut off, two more would grow back in its place! Why do you think Hercules would attempt to defeat this monster when the odds are so against him? Who do you think will prevail?

By putting very light paint next to dark paint, the artist creates a feeling of mystery and suspense. With a single torch to light the room, Hercules' body glows against the murky background, where the evil serpent writhes and hisses in defense. Point to the other places where the light falls. How does this use of light and shadow make the picture dramatic? If this painting came with a soundtrack, what would you hear?

MYTH

SAINT GEORGE KILLING THE DRAGON

Bernardo Martorell

Slayers of dragons and rescuers of damsels in distress seem destined to become heroes. In this picture myth meets reality in a classic tale of good versus evil. Although Saint George really lived, his fire-breathing enemy is the stuff legends are made of. Like the Greek kylix, this picture depicts a hero and his horse battling a fearsome beast. But how are the two artworks different? George is a picture of calm while his foe snarls with fury. Why do you think the saint is so cool?

In addition to the action, the artist uses color to bring the picture to life. Like the jewels in the princess's crown, vivid colors practically jump off the picture. The artist uses certain colors, such as red, to tie the front, middle, and back of the picture together. To see how he did this, trace your finger from the dragon's tongue to the princess's robes to the red objects in the background. What other colors repeat in this way? In a picture so full of color, why do you think the artist dressed his hero in black and white?

MYTH

JOHN HENRY ON THE RIGHT, STEAM DRILL ON THE LEFT

Palmer Hayden

Like Saint George, John Henry was a real person who did things that most people wouldn't even attempt. The legend of John Henry goes like this: working as a steel driver for a railroad company, he was challenged to a match—his hammer versus a steam drill. In the end, John Henry was victorious, and his story was passed down from generation to generation, making him a folk hero along the way. In the picture on this page, the competition is in full swing. Even though he's seen from the rear, the artist makes him the center of attention. How does he accomplish this?

MYTH

HIS HAMMER IN HIS HAND

Palmer Hayden

In another painting from the same series, you see the hero alone in the countryside, holding the tool that made him a legend. In real life, John Henry was only slightly over six feet tall, but here he takes up most of the picture space, making him look larger than life. In what other ways does the artist show you his enormous physical strength? Striding proudly down the tracks, he seems about to walk right out of the picture. Where do you think he is heading? If you could ask him one question, what would it be?

HISTORY

DAVID

Michelangelo

Throughout history there have been many heroes and heroines whose stories live on through time. Many of those stories are told in the Bible. One of the greatest biblical heroes is David, the Hebrew youth who slew the giant Goliath using only his wits and a slingshot. Here David stands eighteen feet tall. It's plain to see that he is naked. Why would the artist choose to show this young hero so tall and without any clothes? With a slingshot draped over his left shoulder, he stares at something only he can see. What do you think he's looking at? Look closely at his steady gaze, penetrating eyes, and furrowed brow. What words would you use to describe this young hero's facial expression? What thoughts could be going through his mind at this moment?

Instead of showing the youth in the act of killing the giant, or just afterward, as other artists have done, this artist chose to show the young hero before the slaying. Because he's not *doing* anything, the artist used contrast, or opposites, to create a feeling of suspense. So while David's body is relaxed, his face is active with thought. One side of his body is at rest, while the other is ready for action. Do you think he'll be prepared for Goliath when the giant arrives?

MOONWALK

Andy Warhol

Sometimes, the hardest and most heroic acts are those that have never been done before. One of the most famous firsts in recent history was the day that man walked on the moon. Imagine taking that first step on an unknown surface with only a few layers of fabric protecting you from the bitter cold, and just an oxygen tank to help you breathe in an atmosphere free of oxygen. Courage was needed, yes, but what other qualities do you think the first men had that allowed them to make that first step? In this picture, you see astronaut Buzz

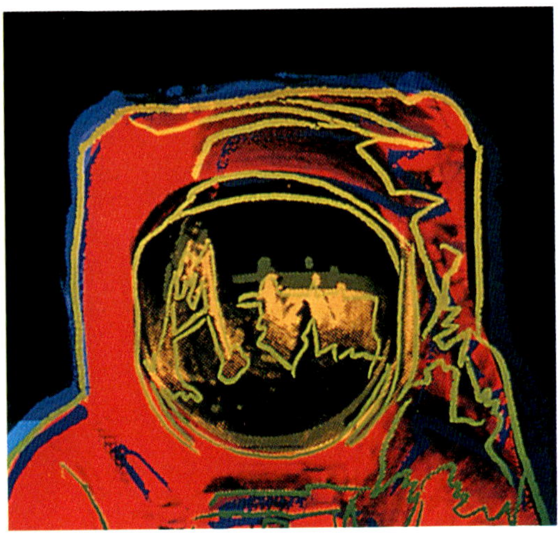

Aldrin standing next to the American flag. Clothed in his spacesuit and helmet, his face is concealed behind a protective shield. What expression do you think he had on his face at that moment? How would you feel if you were inside this spacesuit on the moon?

The artist who made this picture based it on the famous photograph of this moment and changed it with lines and colors. The astronaut's once pure white spacesuit is now

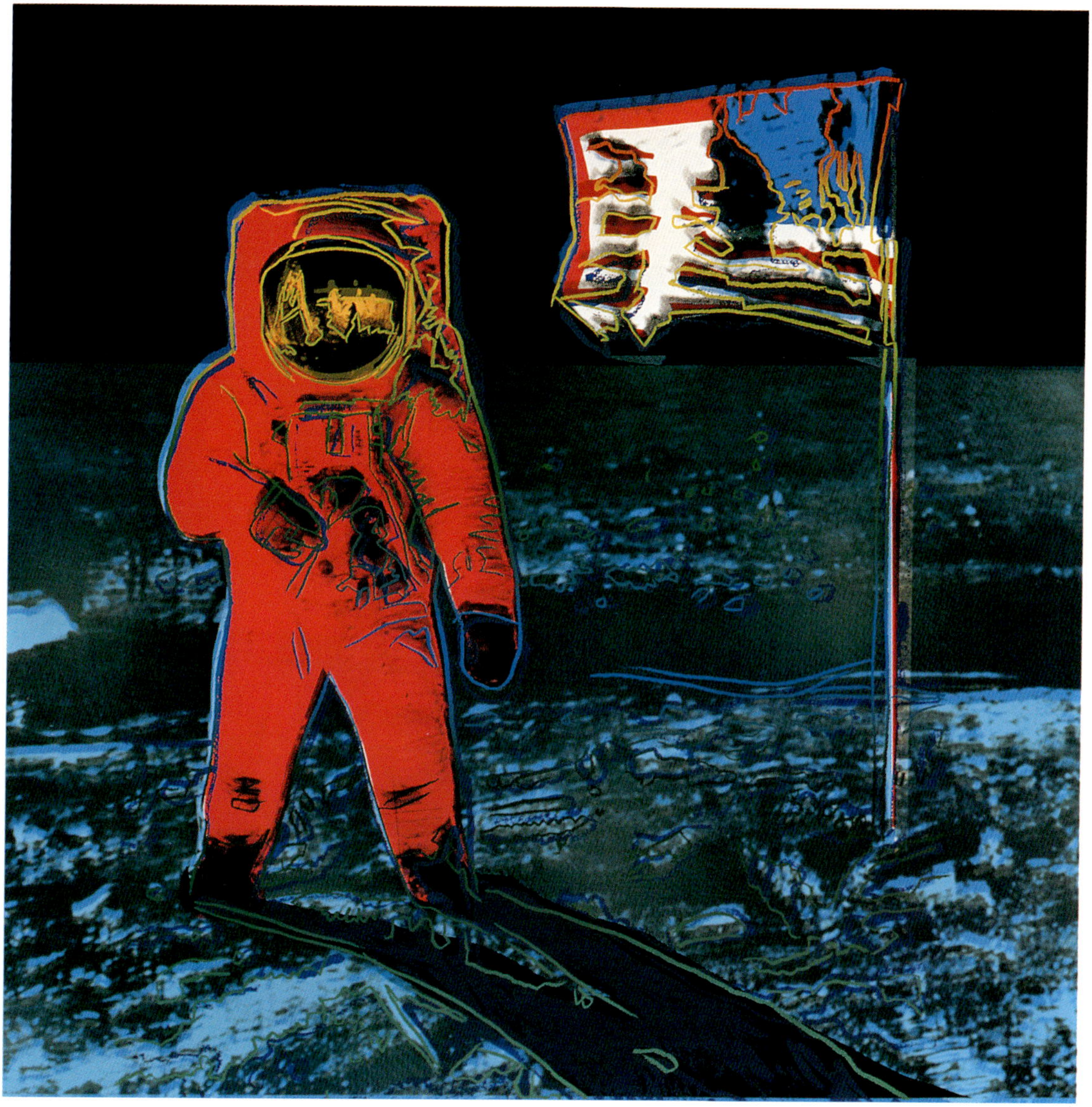

a vivid red, the moon's gray surface a neon blue, and the flag sports bright yellow along with its red, white, and blue. Why do you think the artist would alter reality in this way? How do the colors capture the spirit of this amazing event?

AVGVSTINVS TRINCIVS IACOBVS BVCCA BELLA
CAESAR DE MAGISTRIS CONSERVATORES CVR

HISTORY

EQUESTRIAN STATUE OF MARCUS AURELIUS

Ancient Roman Equestrian Sculpture

History has had many leaders, but only a handful of heroic ones. This statue of the Roman emperor Marcus Aurelius is a monument to his greatness. Astride a beautiful horse, he sits strong and regal, perhaps just having returned to Rome after a military victory. Imagine standing in a crowd of people as he makes his way along the city streets. With one hand outstretched and the other at his side, he seems to be greeting the citizens of Rome who've come to welcome him home. Imagine he stares directly at you. How would it feel to be in his presence?

In life Marcus Aurelius held supreme power over the Roman Empire. To show the "everyday" side of this important person, the artist used many details to make him appear more like someone's father or teacher than the powerful leader of an empire. What details do you see that give him a kind, down-to-earth quality? Wearing only a blanket instead of a saddle, even his horse seems not the mount of an emperor. Why do you think the artist would choose to show a leader like Marcus Aurelius in this way, rather than as an imposing general?

STUDY FOR MARTIN LUTHER KING, JR. MONUMENT

John Wilson

Here you see the great civil rights leader Martin Luther King, Jr., depicted in two ways by the same artist. On this page is a charcoal sketch that the artist drew as a study for what would become the final bronze sculpture. Like the sculptor of the statue of Marcus Aurelius, this artist has tried to capture the deep humanity of a man who helped make the world a better place. The face is finely drawn, while the body is sketched loosely and without much form. King looks directly at you with lips slightly apart, as if he were about to speak. If the drawing could come to life, what might he say?

MARTIN LUTHER KING, JR. MONUMENT

John Wilson

And here is the sculpture that completes the process the artist began with the sketch on the opposite page. If the sketch shows the artist's inspiration, the final work shows the choices he made to get the piece exactly right. In what ways did the artist's early ideas change along the way? Besides the materials that he used for each work, what differences do you see between drawing and sculpture? Which one do you think better expresses the spirit and ideals of this beloved and respected man?

I. INGRES
1854
et son bucher se change
dans les cieux
Deschamps

JOAN OF ARC ON CORONATION OF CHARLES VII IN THE CATHEDRAL OF REIMS

Jean-Auguste-Dominique Ingres

Throughout time, people have gone to war. As horrible as it is, war inspires some people to feats of great heroism. Joan of Arc was one such hero. Her belief in God inspired her to go to war to protect her home and country. Here you see her at the coronation of the king of France. Although she stands in a church and not on the battlefield, she commands respect and awe. How can you tell that she is the most important person in the room? Why do you think the artist chose not to put the king in the painting?

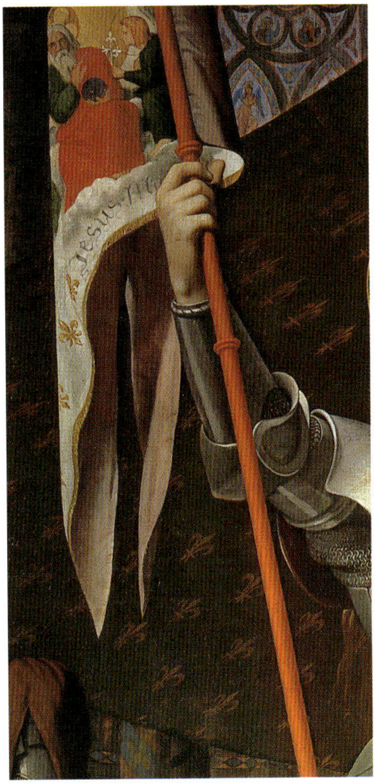

The maid of Orleans is dressed in a suit of armor, a sure sign that she's no ordinary girl. What other details do you see that identify her as a soldier? Like David, Joan of Arc took on a foe much stronger in body than she. How has the artist conveyed her strength of character?

WASHINGTON CROSSING THE DELAWARE

Emanuel Leutze

Before he became the first president of the United States, George Washington led the colonies in the Revolutionary War against England. In this famous painting, Washington and his troops cross the Delaware River on a bitterly cold winter morning. The general stands, his gaze fixed across the river, where the enemy's army is camped. Despite the weather and the battle that lies ahead, Washington seems unfazed. How is his steadfastness a heroic quality? If you were standing before this painting in a museum, you would see that it's huge: twelve feet

high and twenty-one feet wide! Why do you think the artist made the picture so large?

Artists have many ways to get you to see what they want you to see. Here, the most important part of the picture is, of course, General Washington. One way that the artist makes sure you will keep looking at Washington is by using a simple shape — the triangle. To trace this triangle, place your finger at the top of the flagpole, move it to the rear of the boat, then across to the front, and finally back to where you started. Even if you're not aware of it, your eye follows this path as you look at the picture, always falling on General Washington along the way. In what other ways does the artist show his importance?

LIBERTY LEADING THE PEOPLE

Eugene Delacroix

It's easy for artists to depict things that can be seen with the eye, but how can an artist show an idea? One way to do it is by using a person or a thing to represent that idea. In this picture, Liberty becomes a woman. As you look, remind yourself that it's the *idea* of liberty that leads this crowd of French citizens, not an actual person. Holding a bayonet in one hand and the French flag in the other, she spurs the people on despite the horrific happenings on the ground. (One of the people is the artist himself, who painted his self-portrait holding a rifle and wearing a top hat.) In your opinion, who are the heroes in this picture?

Like *Washington Crossing the Delaware,* this painting is quite large, measuring over eight feet high and ten feet wide. It also uses the triangle to move your eye around the main action. The artist packs the picture with drama and movement. The citizen army reaches deep into the background, creating a feeling of great distance. How many people do you think there are? Thick "clouds" hang in the air and create an ominous atmosphere. What do you think these clouds are supposed to be? The main action takes place right up front . . . so close that you are almost part of it, and Liberty and her followers seem about to charge right out of the frame. Imagine that you are part of this group. How do you think it would feel to be caught up in the action?

WAR

THE VIETNAM VETERANS MEMORIAL

Maya Lin

Unfortunately, many war heroes never become subjects of paintings or songs, but remain nameless to most people. And while there are many statues that honor groups of fallen war heroes, how can one statue or monument honor the individual soldier among thousands? In this monument, known as the Wall, the artist created a simple yet moving memorial to all the individual people who died during the Vietnam War or are still missing. Over sixty thousand names are etched into the black stone surface.

People come from far and wide to find the names of their friends and loved ones. How do you think you would feel if you saw the name of someone you knew on the wall? What message do you think the artist is trying to give you about the horrors of war?

Although made by people, the memorial rises out of the ground as if it's a living, growing thing. This was very important to the artist, who wanted the wall to seem like a natural part of the landscape. With its simple shapes, lines, and materials, the monument fits into the park as if it was always there. As you can see, its shiny stone is reflective, like a mirror. What reflections do you see? How do the reflections help the wall blend into the surroundings?

THE LIFE OF A FIREMAN: THE NEW ERA. STEAM AND MUSCLE

Nathaniel Currier and James Merritt Ives

All of the people you've seen so far earned their hero status through acts of courage, heart, and strength, but the ones you are about to see are perhaps the most inspiring of all. Why? Because they are ordinary people doing extraordinary things, such as these New York City firefighters battling a raging fire. The flames dwarf the men, making the odds of getting the blaze under control seem quite small. Do you think they will succeed in putting out this fire? What dangers might befall them at any moment?

As in the picture of Hercules and the Hydra, this picture is full of intensity, action, and drama. And just as Hercules battled the nine-headed serpent, this brigade of hundreds battles a fire that appears too huge to extinguish. The fire leaps across the sky and its smoke joins with the sooty exhaust from the steam engines. Trace your finger along the arc formed by the flames and smoke. Besides adding color and movement to the picture, this line directs your eyes to the action on the street. Look carefully at the firefighters at the bottom of the picture. What tasks are they performing? Who seems to be in charge? If you were one of these brave heroes, what job would you do?

THE PROBLEM WE ALL LIVE WITH

Norman Rockwell

As you've already seen, being the first to attempt something difficult, even dangerous, is indeed heroic. In this picture based on an actual event, a young girl named Ruby Bridges walks into a school that for the very first time was opening its doors to African-American children. Some people were unhappy about the idea of black and white children sharing the same school. Four federal marshals escort Ruby, who stands tall and proud against a backdrop of hate. What details does the artist include that show the racism Ruby faced on this day? If you were in her shoes, how would it make you feel?

As this picture reveals, courage comes in all sizes. Framed by full-grown men, little Ruby's courage and determination towers above them. By choosing not to include the marshalls' heads in the picture, the artist shows you the scene as a child would see it from a short distance away. How does this child's-eye view help you understand what Ruby is experiencing?

THE LIFE LINE

Winslow Homer

Firefighters aren't the only everyday heroes that risk their lives to help others. In this picture, a man holds on to an unconscious woman who is strapped into a rescue contraption called a breeches buoy.
Just inches from the swelling waves, they move along a line known as a hawser.
The wind blows a red cloth over the man's face.
Why would the artist choose to conceal this courageous man's face? If you could see his face, what would his expression look like?

This picture was painted more than a hundred years ago, but it could just as easily be a shot from the latest

Hollywood action movie. Although there are few details in the painting, it is alive with emotion. Placing the people in the center of the picture surrounded by ocean, the artist forces you to focus on the heroic rescue. Without giving you a clue about how far they are from land, a lifeboat, or another ship, the artist leaves it up to you to make up the ending of this thrilling story. If this painting *were* made into a movie, how would this scene end? Why?

EVERYDAY

ALI VS. SONNY LISTON

Neil Leifer

You might not consider a world-famous athlete to be an everyday hero. But like all heroes, professional athletes start out life as regular folks and work very hard to become the best in their sport. One such sports hero is Muhammad Ali, seen here in what has been called the greatest sports photograph of the 20th century. In this image, Ali has just knocked out his opponent. How has the photographer captured the strength, power, and determination of his subject? Like some of the heroes you've already seen, Ali stands victorious against a lone opponent while crowds of people look on. Look back through the pictures in the book. Which ones remind you of this photograph? What qualities do you think this great athlete has in common with those other heroes?

EVERYDAY

ALI IN ZAIRE

Neil Leifer

The best sports heroes are heroic in their everyday lives as well as in competition. In this photograph of Ali in Africa, the love and respect felt for the man is easy to see. By placing him in the middle of the frame, the photographer makes him the center of attention. Balanced on both sides by adoring fans, he leads the crowd with confidence and authority, showing how one person can inspire so many. What other heroes in the book inspire you?

Now that you've seen how some artists see heroes, what do you think it takes to be a hero? Which of these heroic qualities do you have?

NOTE TO PARENTS AND TEACHERS

As an elementary school teacher I had the opportunity to show my students many examples of great art. I was always amazed by their enthusiastic responses to the colors, shapes, subjects, and fascinating stories of the artists' lives. It wasn't uncommon for us to spend an entire class period looking at and talking about just one work of art. By asking challenging questions, I prompted the children to examine and think very carefully about the art, and then quite naturally they would begin to ask all sorts of interesting questions of their own. These experiences inspired me to write this book and the other volumes in the *How Artists See* series.

How Artists See is designed to teach children about the world by looking at art, and about art by looking at the world through the eyes of great artists. The books encourage children to look critically, answer—and ask—thought-provoking questions, and form an appreciation and understanding of an artist's vision. Each book is devoted to a single subject so that children can see how different artists have approached and treated the same theme, and begin to understand the importance of individual style.

Because I believe that children learn most successfully in an atmosphere of exploration and discovery, I've included questions that encourage them to formulate ideas and responses for themselves. And because people's reactions to art are based on their own personal aesthetic, most of the questions are open-ended and have more than one answer. If you're reading aloud to your children or students, give them ample time to look at each work and form their own opinions; it certainly is not necessary to read the whole book in one sitting. Like a good book or movie, art can be enjoyed over and over again, each time with the possibility of revealing something that wasn't seen before.

You may notice that dates and other historical information are not included in the main text. I purposely omitted this information in order to focus on the art and those aspects of the world it illustrates. For children who want to learn more about the artists whose works appear in the book, short biographies are provided at the end, along with suggestions for further reading and a list of museums where you can see additional works by each artist.

After reading *How Artists See Heroes,* children can do a wide variety of related activities to extend and reinforce all that they've learned. In addition to the simple activities I've suggested throughout the main text, they can read biographies of the heroes seen in the book or other heroes of interest, draw a portrait of a favorite hero, or write and perform a short skit featuring their personal heroes. Since the examples shown here are just a tiny fraction of the great works of art that feature heroes as their subject, children can go on a scavenger hunt through museums, your local library, or the Internet to find other images of heroes.

I hope that you and your children or students will enjoy reading and rereading this book and, by looking at many styles of art, discover how artists share with us their unique ways of seeing and depicting our world.

ARTISTS' BIOGRAPHIES

(in order of appearance)

If you'd like to know more about the artists in this book, here's some information to get you started:

THE BOREAD PAINTER, Active: 575 B.C.–550 B.C., *pp. 4–5*

This ancient Greek painter worked for only twenty-five years painting scenes from Greek myths and elaborate decorations on cups and other pottery, but his skill and style has lived on for thousands of years. He lived in the Greek city-state of Sparta, where he operated a pottery workshop. Using the black-figure technique, he would paint the characters and decorations in black glaze on a cup or vase, and then use a finely pointed stylus to etch in the details, revealing the terracotta color of the clay beneath. Like most ancient artists, his actual name is unknown. He is named for a cup historians believe he decorated depicting a scene from the life of Boreas, ancient god of the north wind.

FRANCISCO DE ZURBARÁN (1598–1664), *pp. 6–7*

When the Spanish artist Francisco de Zurbarán (pronounced zur-bah-RAHN) was sixteen years old, his parents sent him off to apprentice in a painter's workshop. At age eighteen, he made a painting of the Immaculate Conception, his earliest known work. Like many artists of this period, he was influenced by the work of the great Renaissance artist Michelangelo Buonarrotti, and his figures have the same three-dimensional, sculptural quality as the Italian master's. He spent the better part of his career painting religious scenes for church leaders and decorating churches and chapels. While he did paint some portraits and still-life pictures, he is mainly known for his dramatic and simple pictures of saints; his series of paintings depicting the labors of Hercules was a detour for this devout painter of Christian themes.

BERNARDO MARTORELL (1400–1452), *pp. 8–9*

This Spanish painter worked in the early part of the Italian Renaissance (see Michelangelo Buonarotti), but his brightly colored, finely detailed paintings have more in common with art of the earlier medieval period. In addition to painting, he produced miniature pictures similar to the illustrations in illuminated manuscripts. He worked in Barcelona and was quite well known as a master painter. The painting featured in this book is one of the few by Martorell that still exist.

PALMER HAYDEN (1890–1973), *pp. 10–11*

Palmer Hayden (also known as Peyton Cole Hedgeman) was born in Virginia toward the end of the nineteenth century and became one of the most respected African-American painters of the twentieth century. As a boy, he liked to draw and listen to stories about John Henry, the folk hero who would later be the subject of his most important paintings. At the start of World War I, Hayden enlisted in the army, where his commanding officer could not pronounce his given name and began calling him Palmer

Hayden, a name he decided to keep. After the war, he moved to New York City and began his formal art studies. It was during the Harlem Renaissance, a period of great artistic achievements by African-Americans. Soon he won a grant to study art in Paris. After returning to New York, Hayden worked as a painter for the United States government. He became more and more interested in painting pictures of African-American life. At the time some people considered his pictures cartoonlike and demeaning to black people. His most famous works, the John Henry Series, took him ten years to complete and brought him praise and respect as a painter. Since his death, his work has been the subject of many museum and gallery exhibitions all over the United States.

MICHELANGELO BUONARROTI (1475–1564), *pp. 12–13*

Michelangelo Buonarroti (pronounced mik-el-AN-jel-loe bwoe-nuh-Roh-tee) was perhaps the most remarkable and gifted artist who ever lived. Born in Florence, Italy, he became an artist's apprentice at thirteen. One year later the teenager was invited to live in the palace of Lorenzo de'Medici, a wealthy businessman and patron of the arts. In his early twenties he began work on a sculpture that he claimed would be "the most beautiful work in marble which exists today in Rome." When he finished the *Pieta,* a beautiful statue of the Virgin Mary holding the dead body of Jesus on her lap, Michelangelo became an overnight star. A short time later, he produced *David,* the sculpture seen in this book, once again stunning people with his ability. He believed that with his chisel he could "release" his sculptures from their stone prison. Because he accepted many difficult projects during his career, he left many works unfinished, and it is possible to see some of these sculptures still partially "trapped" inside the blocks of stone. Although he preferred sculpting to painting, he accepted Pope Julius II's offer to paint the ceiling of the Vatican's Sistine Chapel with scenes from the Bible. After only four years, working almost entirely alone, he completed his masterpiece—one of the greatest works of art ever made. All of this master's art depicts human beings, both men and women, as muscular and powerful; Michelangelo believed that physical strength expressed the strength of the soul.

ANDY WARHOL (1928–1987), *p. 14–15*

"If you want to know everything about me, just look at the surface of my paintings, it's all there, there's nothing more." The American Pop Art painter who said these words was born in Pennsylvania to immigrant parents. As a young man, he found work as a commercial illustrator. In the early 1960s he began to create works of art with subjects borrowed from the world of advertising. Warhol (pronounced WAR-hall) transformed common products such as soap boxes and soup cans into fine art. His work seemed outrageous at the time, yet it propelled Warhol to fame and fortune. Throughout the 1960s, most of his subjects were celebrities, such as movie stars, rock musicians, and world leaders. In addition to painting, Warhol was a printmaker, a filmmaker, and even a magazine publisher. Never one to believe that fame can last forever, he once said, "Everyone will be famous for fifteen minutes," but his groundbreaking art made Warhol one of the most famous and unforgettable artists of the late twentieth century.

ANCIENT ROMAN SCULPTURE, *pp. 16–17*

The subject of a military leader on horseback was a popular one dating back to Ancient Greece. Although the artist of this particular statue is unknown, it is the only one that survives from antiquity, because the papacy in Rome believed it was a portrait of the Christian emperor Constantine. If they had known that it depicted the emperor Marcus Aurelius, it probably would have been destroyed as a symbol of pagan Roman art. In 1537, under orders from the Pope, Michelangelo reluctantly supervised its relocation from its original site to where it resides today. This elegant statue has been the model for many equestrian statues throughout history and right up to the present day.

JOHN WILSON (Born 1922), *pp. 18–19*

This African-American sculptor, painter, printmaker, illustrator, and teacher was educated in Boston, Paris, and Mexico. His artwork can be seen in many museums and sculpture parks. Wilson has received numerous awards and honors throughout his career, and he is included in the Smithsonian Institution's Archives of American Art. Of his sketch for the Martin Luther King, Jr., sculpture in the United States Capitol Building, he said, "I wasn't concerned with getting a photographic likeness, but rather a universal significance. I wanted people to be moved by the sense of this man's connection to humanity." Wilson lives and works in Massachusetts.

JEAN-AUGUSTE-DOMINIQUE INGRES (1780–1867), *pp. 20–21*

As a child, the French artist Jean-Auguste-Dominique Ingres (pronounced AN-gr[uh]), was a gifted artist, and began art school at age eleven. At age seventeen, he started studying with the leader of the Neoclassical painters, artists who were influenced by the beliefs and ideas of Ancient Greece and Rome. Neoclassicism was the direct opposite of Romaticism, a style favored by his arch rival, Eugene Delacroix (see Delacroix biography). Ingres's attention to detail and fine use of line were two of his strengths. As a young man he won the prestigious Prix de Rome and studied there and in Florence on and off from 1806 to 1841. Today he is known primarily for his portrait paintings (a genre he didn't enjoy doing), history paintings, and female nudes. Along with Delacroix, Ingres influenced some of the greatest painters of the next century, such as Henri Matisse and Pablo Picasso.

EMANUEL LEUTZE (1816–1868), *pp. 22–23*

Sometimes it doesn't take a great painter to produce a work that captures the hearts and imaginations of generations. Emanuel Leutze (pronounced LOYT-zuh) is not considered an exceptionally gifted painter, but his *George Washington Crossing the Delaware* is arguably the most famous American painting ever created. Leutze was born in Germany and moved to the United States as a boy. In 1841 he returned to Germany and settled in Dusseldorf, where he became a mentor and teacher to American art students who traveled there. In fact, he painted *George Washington Crossing the Delaware* in Dusseldorf, and had it shipped back to America for exhibition. After its instant success, it was engraved and mass-produced in print form, making it known throughout the country and an icon of American history painting. Leutze eventually moved back to the United States, but never produced another painting as successful as "Washington."

EUGENE DELACROIX (1798–1863), *pp. 24–24*

The French painter Eugene Delacroix (pronounced deh-lah-KWAH) once said, "The source of genius is imagination alone, the refinement of the senses that sees what others do not see, or sees them differently." Born in France toward the end of the eighteenth century, Delacroix was orphaned at age sixteen and at eighteen began his art studies in Paris. His first painting was accepted at the Salon, a very important place where painters sought to exhibit their work. Unlike his arch rival, Ingres, Delacroix worked in the Romantic style, and believed the most important elements of a painting were color, movement, and emotion. His paintings, known for bold color, swirling lines, and dramatic and violent subject matter, made him one of the most important painters of his generation (Ingres was the other). In fact, color was so important to him that he once said, "The work of a painter who is not a colorist is illumination rather than painting . . . color gives the appearance of life." He was greatly influenced by Michelangelo and Peter Paul Rubens, and a trip to northern Africa in 1832 introduced him to the sights and styles of the Arab world. Delacroix used his imagination and genius to create over 850 paintings, thousands of prints and drawings, and many journals, and to indeed see, and paint, the world differently.

MAYA LIN (Born 1959), *pp. 26–27*

The daughter of an artist and a literature professor, Chinese-American architect and sculptor Maya Lin was encouraged as a child to explore ideas and create art. While she was still a senior at Yale University's school of architecture, her design for a Vietnam veteran's memorial to be built in Washington, D.C., was chosen among 1,400 entries, and thrust her into the public eye at age twenty-one. She went on to graduate school to continue her studies in architecture. After that she opened her own design firm in New York City and began receiving commissions from all over the country to design buildings and memorials. Lin strives to create art and architecture that works in harmony with the natural environment. She has said that it is her "desire to completely integrate a work with its site, revealing the connectedness of art to landscape or landscape as art." Lin considers herself both "an architect and artist" who draws inspiration for her works from Japanese garden design, Hopi Indian earth mounds, and the earth artists of the 1960s and 1970s. She lives in New York City and Colorado with her husband and children.

NATHANIEL CURRIER (1813–1895) JAMES MERRITT IVES (1824–1895), *pp. 28–29*

These publishers of "cheap and popular prints" are now household names, but they didn't start life or business together. Nathaniel Currier was born in Massachusetts and when still a teenager worked as a printmaker's assistant. James Ives was born in New York City and was interested in art and learning. Currier purchased the printing business from his employer in 1834, and shortly thereafter achieved acclaim with his print of a steamboat disaster. In 1852 he hired Ives to be his bookkeeper, but the new employee's knowledge of art and savvy business skills brought the business even more success than it had enjoyed before his arrival. Five years later, Currier and Ives became full partners, and their images of American life, news events, and Christmas scenes made them famous throughout the world. Today, an original Currier and Ives hand-colored lithograph is a sought-after collector's item.

NORMAN ROCKWELL (1894–1978), *pp. 30–31*

If every picture tells a story, the American illustrator Norman Rockwell told hundreds of them during his career. Growing up in New York City, Rockwell was part of a middle-class family whose father would often read classic stories to Norman and his siblings; later these stories would influence his art. He began working as an illustrator at age sixteen, and over the next six years became more and more in demand by many popular magazines, such as the *Saturday Evening Post.* Because most of his illustrations were featured in books, magazines, and newspapers, many people saw his work. Readers looked forward to his sweet and funny scenes of everyday life—children playing, people working, and family holidays—and became familiar with the likable cast of characters, many of whom were friends and neighbors of the artist. Although Rockwell's work has often been criticized for being too sweet and sentimental, his paintings and drawings are among the most popular and loved works of American art.

WINSLOW HOMER (1836–1910), *pp. 32–33*

The American artist Winslow Homer was born in New England but moved to New York City as a young man to become an illustrator.When the Civil War broke out, Homer was hired by a popular magazine to paint pictures of the front.After the war he continued making illustrations but spent more and more time painting scenes from everyday life in the realistic style he is known for.In 1881 he traveled to England,where he lived in a seaside fishing village,an experience that took his art in a new direction.When he returned to America he began to paint —in both watercolors and oils —rugged pictures of the sea.He liked to use watercolor paints to sketch scenes from nature,especially the seaside,and he used some of these watercolor studies as ideas for his oil paintings.Winslow Homer is one of America 's most beloved artists because he was able to capture the spirit and beauty of a young nation in his art.

NEIL LEIFER (Born 1942), *pp. 34–35*

This American photographer, photojournalist, and filmmaker grew up loving sports. When he was a teenager, one of his pictures was published in *Sports Illustrated* magazine, thus beginning a career that has taken him to some of the world's most important sporting events, such as the Olympics, the Kentucky Derby, the World Series, and countless boxing matches, where he would often photograph his favorite subject, Muhammad Ali. In addition to *Sports Illustrated,* his work has appeared on the covers and pages of many popular magazines, including *Time, LIFE,* and *Newsweek*. Today Leifer devotes most of his time to filmmaking. He lives and works in New York City.

SUGGESTIONS FOR FURTHER READING

The following children's titles are excellent sources for learning more about the artists profiled in this book:

FOR EARLY READERS (AGES 4–7)

Venezia, Mike. *Eugène Delacroix.* Getting to Know the World's Greatest Artists series. Chicago: Children's Press, 2003.
Romantic painter Eugène Delacroix is the subject of this volume in the popular series that combines factual information, humorous illustrations, and color reproductions to introduce young children to art history. (Also included in this series is *Norman Rockwell,* published September 2000.)

FOR INTERMEDIATE READERS (AGES 8-10)

Bolton, Linda. *Art Revolutions: Pop Art.* Art Revolutions series. New York: Peter Bedrick Books, 2000.
Andy Warhol and many of the other artists who defined the style known as Pop Art are introduced throughout this book, which is part of a series devoted to important movements in modern art.

Gherman, Beverly. *Norman Rockwell: Storyteller with a Brush.* New York: Atheneum, 2000.
This large-format volume introduces readers to the life and long career of illustrator Norman Rockwell with full-color reproductions of his art work and photographs of the man at work and at home.

Hart, Tony. *Michelangelo.* Illustrated by Susan Hellard. Famous Children series. Hauppauge, New York: Barron's Juveniles, 1994.
This cute book introduces young readers to the Renaissance master when he was a budding artist.

Malone, Mary. *Maya Lin: Artist and Architect.* People to Know series. Berkeley Heights, New Jersey: Enslow Publishers, 1995.
A biography of the Chinese-American architect of the Vietnam Veterans Memorial in Washington, D.C.

FOR ADVANCED READERS (AGES 11+)

Beneduce, Ann Keay. *A Weekend with Winslow Homer.* New York: Rizzoli, 1993.
This informative and clever book takes the reader back in time to meet the American painter, who narrates the story of his life and work.

Milande, Veronique. *Michelangelo and His Times.* W5 series. New York: Henry Holt and Company, 1996.
Engaging text, beautiful full-color photographs, and illustrations take readers through the many fascinating stages of the Renaissance master's long and productive life.

WHERE TO SEE THE ARTISTS' WORK

BLACK FIGURE VASE PAINTING (ANCIENT GREECE)

- Acropolis Museum, Athens
- Archeological Museum, Olympia, Greece
- The British Museum, London
- John Paul Getty Museum, Los Angeles
- Louvre Museum, Paris
- Museo Nazionale Romano delle Terme, Rome
- The Metropolitan Museum of Art, New York
- National Gallery of Victoria, Melbourne, Australia
- Staatliche Antikensammlungen und Glyptothek, Munich
- Vatican Museum, Rome
- http://www.getty.edu/art/collections/subjects/s38.htm/

MICHELANGELO BUONAROTTI

- Accademia, Florence
- Bargello, Florence
- Casa Buonarotti, Florence
- Isabella Stewart Gardner Museum, Boston
- The Hermitage, St. Petersburg, Russia
- Louvre Museum, Paris
- Medici Chapel, Florence
- The Metropolitan Museum of Art, New York
- Sistine Chapel, Vatican, Rome
- Uffizi, Florence
- http://www.michelangelo.com/buon/bio-index2.html
- http://cgfa.sunsite.dk/michelan/

CURRIER AND IVES

- Colorado Springs Fine Arts Center, Colorado
- The Corcoran Gallery of Art, Washington, D.C.
- Fine Arts Museums, San Francisco, California
- Museum of the City of New York, New York
- Oakland Museum of California, Oakland
- Strong Museum, Rochester, New York
- The University of Arizona Museum of Art, Tucson
- Woodcock Museum, St. Louis, Missouri
- Worcester Art Museum, Worcester, Massachusetts
- www.currierandives.com

EUGÈNE DELACROIX

- Albright-Knox Art Gallery, Buffalo, New York
- The Art Institute of Chicago
- The Hermitage, St. Petersburg, Russia
- John Paul Getty Museum, Los Angeles
- Louvre Museum, Paris
- The Metropolitan Museum of Art, New York
- The Minneapolis Institute of Arts, Minneapolis, Minnesota
- Musée d'Orsay, Paris
- Museum of Fine Arts, Boston
- Museum of Fine Arts, Houston
- Nasjonal Galleriet, Oslo, Norway
- National Gallery of Art, Washington, D.C.
- National Gallery, London
- National Gallery, Prague
- National Museum of Western Art, Tokyo

- Walters Art Gallery, Baltimore, Maryland
- http://tigtail.org/L_view/TVM/X2/a.neoClassic/delacroix/delacroix/html/

WINSLOW HOMER

- Addison Gallery of American Art, Phillips Academy, Andover, Massachusetts
- Amon Carter Museum, Fort Worth, Texas
- Brandywine River Museum, Chadds Ford, Pennsylvania
- Butler Institute of American Art, Youngstown, Ohio
- Cummer Museum of Art and Gardens, Jacksonville, Florida
- Everson Museum of Art, Syracuse, New York
- Fogg Art Museum, Harvard University, Cambridge, Massachusetts
- Freer Gallery of Art, Smithsonian Institution, Washington, D.C.
- The Metropolitan Museum of Art, New York
- Montgomery Museum of Fine Arts, Montgomery, Alabama
- National Museum of American Art, Smithsonian Institution, Washington, D.C.
- New Orleans Museum of Art, New Orleans, Louisiana
- North Carolina Museum of Art, Raleigh, North Carolina
- Pennsylvania Academy of Fine Arts, Philadelphia
- Terra Museum of American Art, Chicago, Illinois
- Wichita Art Museum, Wichita, Kansas
- http://www.boston.com/mfa/homer/mfahomer.htm

PALMER HAYDEN

- Countee Cullen Collection, Hampton University Museum, Hampton, Virginia
- Museum of African American Art, Los Angeles
- National Gallery of Art, Washington, D.C.
- National Museum of African Art, Smithsonian Institution, Washington, D.C.
- National Museum of American Art, Smithsonian Institution, Washington, D.C.
- http://www.stanford.edu/~tshih/Hayden.html

JEAN-AUGUSTE-DOMINIQUE-INGRES

- E.G. Bührle Collection, Zurich, Switzerland
- Cleveland Museum of Art, Cleveland, Ohio
- Detroit Institute of Art, Detroit, Michigan
- Frick Collection, New York
- John Paul Getty Museum, Los Angeles
- The Hermitage, St. Petersburg, Russia
- Kunstmuseum Basel, Switzerland
- Louvre Museum, Paris
- Musée d'Orsay, Paris
- National Gallery, London
- National Gallery of Art, Washington, D.C.
- Philadelphia Museum of Art, Philadelphia, Pennsylvania
- San Diego Museum of Art, San Diego, California
- Walters Art Gallery, Baltimore, Maryland
- http://www.artcyclopedia.com/artists/ingres_jean_auguste-dominique.html

NEIL LEIFER

- www.neilleifer.com

EMANUEL LEUTZE

- Corcoran Gallery of Art, Washington, D.C.
- Gilcrease Museum, Tulsa, Oklahoma
- Los Angeles County Museum of Art
- The Metropolitan Museum of Art, New York
- Monmouth County Historical Association, Freehold, New Jersey
- National Gallery of Art, Washington, D.C.
- National Museum of American Art, Smithsonian Institution, Washington, D.C.
- National Portrait Gallery, Smithsonian Institution, Washington, D.C.
- New-York Historical Society, New York
- Reynolda House Museum of American Art, Winston-Salem, North Carolina
- Wadsworth Atheneum Museum of Art, Hartford, Connecticut
- www.virtualmuseum.calExhibitions/Landscapes/m-ig1-e.php3#

MAYA LIN

- Arts on the Point, Boston
- Asian Pacific American Studies Institute, New York University, New York
- Charlotte Coliseum, Charlotte, North Carolina
- Cleveland Public Library, Cleveland, Ohio
- Long Island Railroad, Pennsylvania Station, New York
- The Mall, Washington, D.C.
- Museum for African Art, New York
- Peace Chapel, Juniata College, Huntingdon, Pennsylvania
- Rockefeller Foundation, New York
- Southern Poverty Law Center, Montgomery, Alabama
- University of Michigan, Ann Arbor
- Wexner Center for the Arts, Ohio State University, Columbus, Ohio
- Yale University, New Haven, Connecticut
- http://womensearlyart.net/lin/lin.html

BERNARDO MARTORELL

- The Art Institute of Chicago
- Collection Lippmann, Berlin
- Gerona Museum, Spain
- Louvre Museum, Paris
- Montreal Museum of Fine Arts, Quebec
- Santa Creu Cathedral, Barcelona
- http://cgfa.sunsite.dk/m/p-martorell6.html

NORMAN ROCKWELL

- The Brooklyn Museum of Art, New York
- Columbus Museum of Art, Columbus, Ohio
- Delaware Art Museum, Wilmington, Delaware
- Denver Art Museum, Denver, Colorado
- High Museum of Art, Atlanta, Georgia
- Los Angeles County Museum of Art
- National Cowboy and Western Heritage Museum, Oklahoma City, Oklahoma
- National Museum of American Illustration, Newport, Rhode Island
- National Portrait Gallery, Washington, D.C.
- New Britain Museum of American Art, New Britain, Connecticut
- Peabody Essex Museum, Salem, Massachusetts
- The John and Mable Ringling Museum of Art, Sarasota, Florida
- Norman Rockwell Museum, Stockbridge, Massachusetts
- Sheldon Memorial Art Gallery and Sculpture Garden, Lincoln, Nebraska

- Society of Illustrators Museum, New York
- Mark Twain Home and Museum, Hannibal, Missouri
- The White House, Washington, D.C.
- http://www.nrm.org/
- http://www.rockwelltour.org/frameset.html

ANDY WARHOL

- Art Gallery of Ontario, Toronto
- The Art Institute of Chicago
- Beyeler Foundation Collection, Riehen, Switzerland
- Butler Institute of American Art, Youngstown, Ohio
- Chrysler Museum, Norfolk, Virginia
- City Museum, Amsterdam
- Davenport Museum of Art, Davenport, Iowa
- Eiteljorg Museum of American Indians and Western Art, Indianapolis, Indiana
- Guggenheim Museum Soho, New York, New York
- Hirshhorn Museum and Sculpture Garden, Smithsonian Institution, Washington, D.C.
- Herbert F. Johnson Museum of Art, Cornell University, Ithaca, New York
- Lowe Art Museum, Coral Gables, Florida
- The Metropolitan Museum of Art, New York
- Museum of Contemporary Art, Chicago
- Museum of Modern Art, New York
- Museum of the Twentieth Century, Vienna
- National Gallery of Art, Washington, D.C.
- The Andy Warhol Museum, Pittsburgh, Pennsylvania
- Whitney Museum of Art, New York
- http://www.artcyclopedia.com/artists/warhol_andy.html

JOHN WILSON

- Bezalel Museum of Fine Arts, Jerusalem, Israel
- Carnegie Institute, Pittsburgh, Pennsylvania
- DeCordova Sculpture Park, Lincoln, Massachusetts
- Museum of African American Art, Los Angeles
- Museum of Fine Arts, Boston
- Museum of Modern Art, New York
- Smith College Museum of Art, Northampton, Massachusetts
- United States Capitol Building, Rotunda, Washington, D.C.

FRANCISCO DE ZURBARÁN

- Academy of San Fernando, Seville, Spain
- Alte Pinakothek, Munich
- Cleveland Museum of Art, Cleveland, Ohio
- Louvre, Paris
- Musée Fabre, Montpellier
- Museum of Fine Arts, Budapest, Hungary
- Museum of Fine Arts, Seville, Spain
- National Gallery, London
- Norton Simon Museum, Pasadena, California
- Prado Museum, Madrid
- Provincial Museum, Cadiz
- Pushkin Museum, Moscow
- Shaw Collection, Buenos Aires
- http://www.kfki.hu/~arthp/html/z/zurbaran/index.html

CREDITS *(listed in order of appearance)*

The Boread Painter (active: 575 B.C.–550 B.C.). *Black Figure Kylix,* c. 570 B.C–565 B.C. Terracotta, 5 x 7 1/8 in. (12.5 x 18.5 cm). The J. Paul Getty Museum, Malibu, California. Photo: Ellen Rosenbery. Francisco de Zurbarán (1598–1664). *Struggle of Hercules with the Hydra of Lerna,* c. 1598–1664. Oil on canvas, 52 x 38 in. (133 x 167 cm). Museo del Prado. © Scala/Art Resource, New York. Bernardo Martorell. *Saint George Killing the Dragon,* c. 1438. Tempera on panel, 61.1 x 38.5 in. (155.3 x 98 cm). © 2002 The Art Institute of Chicago; Gift of Mrs. Richard E. Danielson and Mrs. Chauncey McCormick. Palmer Hayden (1890–1973). *John Henry on the Right, Steam Drill on the Left,* 1944–47. Oil on canvas, 30 x 40 in. (76.23 x 101.64 cm). Museum of African American Art, Los Angeles. *His Hammer in His Hand,* 1944–47. Oil on canvas, 30 x 40 in. (76.23 x 101.64 cm). Museum of African American Art, Los Angeles; Gift of Miriam Hayden. Michelangelo (1475–1564). *David,* 1502–1503. Marble, height: 170.8 in. (434 cm). Galleria dell'Accademia. Photo: Takashi Okamura/Art Resource, New York. Andy Warhol (1928–1989). *Moonwalk,* 1987. Printed on Lenox Museum Board (one from a portfolio of two screenprints), 38 x 38 in. (96.5 x 96.5 cm). © The Andy Warhol Foundation for the Visual Arts/Art Resource. © Artist Rights Society, New York. Unknown Sculptor (Ancient Roman). *Equestrian Statue of Marcus Aurelius.* Bronze, 11 ft. 6 in. (350.6 cm). Camidoglio, Rome, Italy. © Scala/Art Resource, New York. John Wilson (1922–). *Study for Martin Luther King, Jr.,* 1981. Charcoal on paper, 28.5 in x 28 in. (72.4 x 71.1 cm). Courtesy VAGA, New York. *Martin Luther King, Jr. Monument* (Sculpture for the United States Capitol, Washington, D.C.), final bronze: 1985; unveiled: 1986. Bronze, 36 x 17.75 x 30.5 in. (91.4 x 45.1 x 77.5 cm). Courtesy of VAGA, New York. Jean Auguste Dominique Ingres (1778–1867). *Joan of Arc on Coronation of Charles VII in Cathedral of Reims,* 1854. Oil on canvas, 94.5 x 70 in. (240 x 178 cm). © The Louvre, Paris/Art Resource, New York. Photo: Erich Lessing. Emanuel Leutze (1816–1848). *Washington Crossing the Delaware,* 1851. Oil on canvas, 149 x 255 in. (378.5 x 647.7 cm). The Metropolitan Museum of Art; Gift of John Stewart Kennedy 1897. © 1992 The Metropolitan Museum of Art. Eugene Delacroix (1798–1863). *Liberty Leading the People,* 1830. Oil on canvas, 102 x 127.9 in. (260 x 325 cm). © Reunion des Musees Nationaux/Art Resource, New York. Photo: Herve Lewandowski. Maya Lin (1959–) *The Vietnam Veterans Memorial,* groundbreaking: March 26, 1982; dedication: November 1982. Black granite, length of each wall: 46 ft. 9 in. (75.21 m); total length: 493 ft. 6 in. (150.4 m); height at center: 10 ft. 3 in. (3.12 m); angle: 125 degrees, 12 ft. Photographed: November 10, 1982. © Corbis/Bettman. Photo: Joyce Naltchayan, AFP/Corbis. Nathaniel Currier (1813–1895) and James Merrill Ives (1824–1895). *The Life of a Fireman: The New Era. Steam and Muscle,* 1861. Lithograph, 19.2 x 25.8 in. (48.7 x 65.6 cm). Museum of the City of New York. The J. Clarence Davies Collection. Norman Rockwell (1894–1978). *The Problem We All Live With,* Completed for *Look* for the January 14, 1964 issue. Oil on canvas, 36 x 58 in. (91.5 x 147.3 cm). Collection of the Norman Rockwell Museum, Stockbridge, Massachusetts. Winslow Homer (1836–1910). *The Life Line,* 1884. Oil on canvas, 28 2/5 x 44 3/4 in. (72.7 x 113.7 cm). Philadelphia Museum of Art: George W. Elkins Collection. Neil Leifer (1942–). *Ali vs. Sonny Liston,* May 25, 1965. Photographed with a 2 1/4 chrome. © Neil Leifer. *Ali in Zaire ,* 1974. Photographed with 35 mm film. © Neil Leifer.